BRENT LIBRARIES

Please return/renew this item
by the last date shown.
Books may also be renewed by
phone or online.
Tel: 0115 929 3388
On-line www.brent.gov.uk/libraryservice

THE ARAB–ISRAELI CONFLICT

Nicola Barber

W
FRANKLIN WATTS
LONDON · SYDNEY

Paperback edition first published in 2014 by Franklin Watts

Franklin Watts
338 Euston Road
London
NW1 3BH

 Franklin Watts Australia
Level 17/207 Kent Street, Sydney, NSW 2000

Produced by Arcturus Publishing Limited,
26/27 Bickels Yard, 151–153 Bermondsey Street, London SE1 3HA

Editors: Nicola Barber and Joe Harris
Picture researcher: Nicola Barber
Designer: Ian Winton

Picture credits:
Corbis: cover left and 28 (Peter Turnley), title page and 17 (Hulton-Deutsch Collection),
11 (Bettmann), 13 (Bettmann), 14 (Bettmann), 19 (David Rubinger), 21 (Christian Simonpietri/Sygma),
23 (Bettmann), 25 (Bettmann), 27 (Alain Keler/Sygma), 31 (Richard T. Nowitz), 42 (Alon Ron/Pool/epa).
Shutterstock: cover right (Ryan Rodrick Beiler), 7 (J van der Wolf), 9 (Arkady Mazor), 33 (Ryan Rodrick Beiler),
35 (zebra0209), 37 (Ryan Rodrick Beiler), 39 (Ryan Rodrick Beiler), 40 (Ryan Rodrick Beiler).

British Library Cataloguing in Publication Data

Barber, Nicola.
   The Arab–Israeli conflict. -- (Both sides of the story)
   1. Arab–Israeli conflict--Juvenile literature.
   I. Title II. Series.
   956'.04-dc23

 ISBN: 978 1 4451 3019 4

Franklin Watts is a division of Hachette Children's Books, an Hachette UK company.
www.hachette.co.uk

Printed in China

Supplier 03, Date 0913 Print Run 2949
SL001560EN

Contents

What are the Historical Claims?

For over 100 years there has been conflict between Arabs and Jews in the Middle East. This conflict is essentially over land, and who has the rights to live on it, work it and control it. Palestine, the land at the heart of the conflict, lies at the eastern end of the Mediterranean Sea between the coast and the River Jordan, with the arid Negev region in the south, and Lebanon to the north. In 1948, the State of Israel was created out of Palestine as a homeland for the Jewish people. Why did the Jews claim this land as their own, and what claims did the Arabs make over it?

A holy land

Palestine is often referred to as the Holy Land because it contains holy sites for the Jewish, Christian and Muslim religions. The city of Jerusalem is particularly important as a holy city and a place of pilgrimage. For Jews, the Western (Wailing) Wall is a sacred place where they come to pray. For Christians, Jerusalem is the place where Jesus was tried and crucified. For Muslims, the Dome of the Rock marks the holy place from where the Prophet Muhammad made his night journey to Paradise.

Jewish claims over Palestine

The Jews are a people bound together by religion, culture, language and history. The basis of their claims over Palestine are biblical: according to the Bible, Moses led the Israelites (Jews) out of Egypt and into the 'Promised Land' (Israel). Palestine was the historical site of two Jewish kingdoms, Israel and Judah. However, in 586 BCE, and again in the 1st century CE when Palestine was part of the Roman Empire, many Jews were expelled from their historic homeland and forced to settle elsewhere. This dispersal of Jews is known as the diaspora. The Jews became a scattered people, with only a few thousand remaining in Palestine. But despite the diaspora, many Jews still felt strong religious and cultural ties to the 'Promised Land'.

Arab claims over Palestine

The Arabs are a people who originally came from the Arabian peninsula, and who share a common language and culture. From the 7th century CE many Arabs became followers of the Prophet Muhammad. These Arab Muslims took the new religion of Islam far beyond the Arabian peninsula as they spread across the Middle East (including Palestine) and north Africa.

Jewish worshippers pray at the Western Wall (also known as the Wailing Wall) in Jerusalem, Israel. Beyond the Wall the golden roof of the Dome of the Rock is visible.

However, not all Arabs share the same religious faith: while the majority are Muslim, there are significant numbers of Christian Arabs. Like the Jews, the Palestinian Arabs – both Muslim and Christian – claim that they can trace their ancestors in Palestine far back into history.

Zionism and Arab nationalism

After the diaspora (dispersal), Jews settled in communities scattered across the world. They built synagogues, and kept alive their religious and cultural traditions. But they also frequently encountered persecution. In European countries, where the majority of people were Christians, Jews were often required to live in separate areas. Sometimes communities of Jews were expelled from countries and forced to make their homes elsewhere. This type of anti-Jewish behaviour is known as anti-Semitism.

Zionism

During the 19th century there was a rise in anti-Semitism, particularly in eastern Europe and Russia, where there were large communities of Jews. Many Jewish people fled to western Europe and the USA. A minority of Jews considered another option. In 1896, an Austrian Jew called Theodor Herzl published a book called *The Jewish State* (see panel, page 9). Herzl's book helped to launch Zionism, a political movement aimed at establishing a Jewish homeland in Palestine. Many Jews considered Palestine to be their 'Promised Land' – the Biblical land of Israel. Inspired by the Zionist movement, Jewish settlers began to move to Palestine.

Arab nationalism

Since the 16th century, Arabs across much of the Middle East had been ruled by the Ottoman Turks (who were Muslims, but not Arabs). At the same time as Zionism was gathering pace among the Jewish communities around the world, there was an upsurge in Arab nationalism. The Arabs wanted to be rid of their Turkish masters and to establish independent Arab rule in the Middle East, including Palestine.

There were several Arab uprisings against the Ottoman Empire, but

Historic homeland

'We are a people – one people… Palestine is our unforgettable historic homeland… the Jews who will it shall achieve their State. We shall live at last as free men on our own soil, and in our own homes peacefully die.'

From **The Jewish State,** *Theodor Herzl, 1896*

This old stamp shows the founder of modern Zionism, Theodor Herzl. The stamp was printed in Israel in 1960 to commemorate the 100th anniversary of Herzl's birth.

the turning point in the struggle for Arab independence came during World War I. In this war, the Ottoman Empire fought alongside Germany against Britain and its allies. In 1915, the British secretly made contact with Arab leaders and offered to do a deal (see page 10). If the Arabs would rise up against the Turks, Britain would support Arab independence. The Arabs raised an army, and by 1918 the Ottoman Empire was defeated.

Seeds of dissent

In 1917, Britain declared its support for a Jewish homeland in Palestine. This declaration was made in a letter (see panel, page 11) written by the British Foreign Secretary, Lord Balfour, to a prominent Jewish banker, Lord Rothschild. It is often called the 'Balfour Declaration'. It was the first time that a world power had stated its support for the Zionist cause. The Declaration also appeared to contradict the secret agreement made with the Arabs.

Betrayal

At the end of World War I, the Arabs expected Britain to fulfill its promise of support for Arab independence. But under the terms of another secret agreement (the Sykes-Picot Agreement 1916), Britain and France divided up the former Ottoman lands in the Middle East between them. Britain was given a mandate to rule Palestine, Transjordan (later Jordan) and Iraq until the Arabs were considered ready to govern themselves. France was to control Syria and Lebanon.

The Palestine problem

In Palestine, the British were faced with a dilemma. In the Balfour Declaration they had openly backed the establishment of a Jewish state.

Arab independence

'Great Britain is prepared to recognise and support the independence of the Arabs in all the regions within the limits demanded by the Sherif of Mecca…
I am convinced that this declaration will assure you beyond all possible doubt of the sympathy of Great Britain towards the aspirations [hopes] of her friends the Arabs and will result in a firm and lasting alliance…'

From a letter written by Sir Henry McMahon, the British High Commissioner in Cairo, Egypt, to Ali ibn Husain, the Sherif of Mecca, in 1915 as part of the secret negotiations between the British and the Arabs.

Yet they had also promised the Arabs to support their independence. Many Arabs were increasingly concerned about Jewish settlement in Palestine, and during the 1920s and '30s there were violent clashes between Arabs and Zionist Jews. Britain, meanwhile, tried to please both sides, limiting Jewish immigration into Palestine while refusing to give power to the Arab majority.

It was events in Europe that brought matters to a head. In 1933, Adolf Hitler came to power in Germany. The anti-Semitic policies of his Nazi Party forced thousands of Jews to flee. Some managed to reach Palestine, where tensions with the Arabs increased. In 1936 widespread fighting broke out between Arabs and Jewish settlers in Palestine.

Jewish homeland

'His Majesty's Government view with favour the establishment in Palestine of a national home for the Jewish people, and will use their best endeavours to facilitate the achievement of this object...'

From the 'Balfour Declaration' 1917

Faisal (centre), son of Ali ibn Husain, the Sherif of Mecca, with his advisers at the peace conference that followed the end of World War I. The conference was held in Versailles, Paris, in 1919.

The Jewish State

In 1947, Britain turned to the newly formed United Nations (UN) to try to resolve its problems in Palestine. As details emerged after World War II of the horrors suffered by Jews at the hands of the Nazis (see panel), many people felt the time had come for an independent Jewish state. The UN put forward a plan to partition (divide) Palestine between the Jews and the Arabs, with an international zone around Jerusalem.

Zionist leaders accepted the plan, although they would have preferred to have control over Jerusalem. They decided to use the biblical name Israel for their new state. The Arab leaders, however, rejected the UN proposal because it gave 55 per cent of Palestine to the Jewish people, who formed just 37 per cent of the population and owned 7 per cent of the land.

Bitter fighting broke out once again between Arabs and Jews in Palestine. Many Palestinian Arab families who found themselves living in areas that were due to become part of Israel started to move out of those areas. Both sides fought for control of key roads and supply routes, particularly in and out of Jerusalem.

The Holocaust

In the years leading up to World War II (1939–45), Jews living in Nazi-controlled Germany suffered worsening discrimination and persecution. During the war, the Nazis made a systematic and horrifying attempt to wipe out all the Jews in the countries they controlled. Today, this genocide, in which six million Jews died, is known as the Holocaust.

Deir Yassin

In April 1948, Deir Yassin, an Arab village just outside Jerusalem, was attacked by forces of the Irgun, an extremist Zionist organization. The attackers killed most of the population of the village, including women and children. The reasons for this massacre and exactly what

Arab refugees from a village near Haifa in northern Israel. They left hurriedly in June 1948 carrying only what they could fit into their large bundles.

happened during the attack remain subjects of debate. But the events at Deir Yassin caused general panic and fear among Palestinian Arabs, and many fled as a result.

The refugee question

Thousands of Arabs left their homes in Palestine, around 700,000 by the end of the war in 1948. Some were forcibly expelled by Zionist forces; others left because of fear and intimidation. They went as refugees to other parts of Palestine, and to neighbouring Arab states such as Syria, Transjordan and Lebanon. Some people allege that Arab leaders themselves encouraged people to leave their homes in order to allow Arab fighters to advance more easily. The arguments about why the Palestinian Arabs left, and whether they should be permitted to return, have continued ever since (see pages 40–1).

Victory or catastrophe?

On 14 May 1948, David Ben-Gurion declared Israel's independence and became the first prime minister of the new state. None of the Arab countries surrounding Israel recognized its right to exist. The following day, Israel was invaded by forces from Lebanon, Syria, Iraq, Transjordan and Egypt, turning the civil war between Palestinian Arabs and Jews into a full-blown Arab–Israeli inter-state conflict. The war that followed is today known by Israelis as the War of Independence, and by Palestinian Arabs as the *naqba* – 'catastrophe' or 'disaster'.

David Ben Gurion (centre left, wearing jacket), soon to be the first prime minister of the new state of Israel, bids farewell to the last of the British troops to leave Palestine, in April 1948.

The Israeli army

How did the brand-new state of Israel defend itself against simultaneous attack from five hostile countries? In fact, the Palestinian Jews had long anticipated this fight, and had prepared for it. A military organization, called the Haganah, had been formed in the 1920s to protect Jewish interests in Palestine. The Haganah formed the core of the Israeli army. Many of the Israeli troops were experienced, tough fighters. They were also highly motivated – they were, after all, fighting for the survival of their new state.

Nevertheless, the Israelis were desperately short of soldiers and weapons at the beginning of the war. But during a ceasefire negotiated by the UN in June 1948, Israel managed both to build up its troop numbers and to import large amounts of equipment and weapons from eastern Europe. After this the war swung in Israel's favour, as its army began to capture territories beyond the boundaries of the UN partition.

Divided aims?

What were the aims of the Arab states that invaded Israel in 1948? On the face of it, the battle was to liberate the Arab Palestinians from the Zionists. But the Arab leaders also had ambitions to lay claim to and control parts of Palestine for themselves, rather than establishing an independent Palestinian state. With divided aims, there was little co-ordination between Arab troops from different countries. And although the number of Arab troops roughly matched that of the Israelis, they were mostly less well trained and equipped. By the end of 1948 the Israelis had gained significant amounts of land, and thousands of Palestinian Arabs had become refugees.

After the 1948–9 war

- Israel increased its territory by 22 per cent compared to the land allotted under the UN partition

- Transjordan took control of the West Bank (an area to the west of the river Jordan) and East Jerusalem

- Egypt took control of the Gaza Strip (an area along the coast to the north of the Sinai Peninsula)

- the Palestinian state proposed in the UN partition plan was never established

At War

In 1967, increasing tension between Israel and its Arab neighbours pushed the two sides into a war. The disagreements about who started this war continue to this day. The fighting began on 5 June and lasted just six days, from which the war takes its name, the Six-Day War.

Background to the war

Since 1949, Israel had become an industrialized, modern state. It had built up a highly trained and well-equipped army, which was constantly on the alert for attack from its Arab neighbours. The Arab states remained united in their opposition to Israel, and in 1964 had set up the Palestine Liberation Organization (see pages 22–3), dedicated to winning back the land lost in the 1948–9 war. Crucially, the world's two superpowers were involved in the region, too. Israel received huge amounts of aid from the USA, while the Arab states were supported by the Soviet Union.

Israeli aggression?

'The existence of Israel has continued too long. We welcome the Israeli aggression. We welcome the battle ... The battle has come in which we shall destroy Israel.'

From a broadcast on Cairo Radio, May 1967

Attack or self-defence?

Throughout 1966, there were raids along the borders between Israel and Syria, and Israel and Jordan. In November, Syria and Egypt signed a pact promising to defend each other in case of attack. In Israel, the pact had the effect of heightening the sense of threat all around. Then, in May 1967, the Soviet Union warned Syria that Israel was preparing an attack against its ally, Egypt. Although the information was incorrect, the rumour was enough to make the Egyptian leader, President Abdel Nasser, move thousands of troops into Sinai, the region bordering Israel in the southwest.

At the end of May, Jordan signed a defence pact with Egypt. By this time, war fever had taken hold in some Arab countries, with daily

No aggressive intentions

'Israel wants to make it clear to the government of Egypt that it has no aggressive intentions whatsoever against any Arab state at all.'

Israeli Prime Minister Levi Eshkol, May 1967

threats against Israel in the papers and on the radio.

With all diplomatic attempts to calm the crisis exhausted, on 5 June Israel launched a surprise attack on Egypt. On that first day of the war, the Israelis crippled the Egyptian, Jordanian and Syrian airforces. Six days later, Israel was celebrating a decisive victory.

Israeli soldiers inspect the burnt-out wreckage of an Egyptian aircraft at Al-Arish airport, in Sinai, on 8 June 1967.

The aftermath

Israel emerged victorious at the end of the Six-Day War, but the war brought the region no closer to a resolution of its problems. The bitterness of defeat felt by the Arab states was directed not only at Israel but also at its supporters, notably the USA. At the end of August 1967, at a meeting in Khartoum, Sudan, Arab leaders pledged to continue the fight against the state of Israel with what became known as the 'three noes': '… no peace with Israel, no recognition of Israel, no negotiations with it, and insistence on the rights of the Palestinian people in their own country' (Khartoum Resolutions, 1 September 1967).

New territories

- **West Bank and East Jerusalem:** annexed by Transjordan in 1950 and governed as part of Jordan. West Bank occupied by Israel in 1967, East Jerusalem annexed by Israel in 1967

- **Golan Heights:** mountainous area to the north of the Sea of Galilee. Part of Syria until it was occupied by Israel in 1967

- **Gaza Strip:** occupied by Egypt in 1949, occupied by Israel in 1967

- **Sinai:** large desert area that forms the Sinai peninsula. Part of Egypt until it was occupied by Israel in 1967; returned to Egypt in 1979

Israel's conquests in the Six-Day War expanded its territory by three times. Israel now controlled the West Bank and the Golan Heights in the north, and the Gaza Strip and Sinai in the south. For the first time, Israel also had control of all of the city of Jerusalem. These conquests gave Israel more security as its borders were easier to defend. But it also brought new challenges as around one million Palestinian Arabs living in the West Bank and Gaza Strip came under Israeli administration.

Resolution 242

Immediately after the end of the war, Israel considered withdrawing from the Golan Heights and Sinai in return for peace treaties with Syria and Egypt. But this plan was rejected by Egypt and then quickly withdrawn by the Israelis. Instead, Israel decided on military occupation of its new territories.

A Palestinian child balances a tray of food while walking through a devastated village in the West Bank in 1967.

In November 1967, the UN issued Resolution 242. The resolution called for Israel's withdrawal from 'territories occupied in the recent conflict'. It also stated the right of every state in the area 'to live in peace within secure and recognized boundaries free from threats or acts of force…'. The resolution was open to interpretation on both sides: the Arabs insisted that it called for Israeli withdrawal from *all* occupied territories, while the Israelis claimed the right to hold on to some territories in order to live within 'secure boundaries'.

The October War

In the years following the Six-Day War, Egyptian and Israeli forces frequently clashed in cross-border confrontations in Sinai. Egypt was being supplied with arms and aircraft by the Soviet Union, while the USA continued to support Israel. In September 1970, Anwar Sadat became President of Egypt after the death of Abdel Nasser. In a change of policy, Sadat decided to bring the ongoing conflict with Israel to an end. But negotiations with the Israeli prime minister, Golda Meir, were unsuccessful, despite pressure on Israel from the USA to make a settlement. Boosted by military aid from the USA, Israel felt strong. The Israelis did not believe that Egypt, or any of its Arab allies, were in any position to fight another war.

Yom Kippur

Frustrated by the lack of progress, Sadat decided to go to war. He made secret plans with Syria to attack Israel on two fronts. When the attack came, on 6 October 1973, it was well-planned and rehearsed – and a complete shock for the Israelis. It was Yom Kippur, the Day of Atonement, the holiest day in the Jewish year

The oil weapon

Egypt and Syria had the backing of oil-producing states in the Middle East. In 1973, these states voted to drastically reduce their exports of oil to the West, and to ban exports to the USA and countries in Europe. With supplies restricted, the price of oil rocketed. The oil embargo lasted until 1974 and showed the world that the Arab states had a powerful 'weapon' at their disposal.

and a holiday across Israel. While Egyptian forces moved in from the south, and the Syrian army attacked the Golan Heights, the Israel Defense Forces (IDF) quickly mobilized. In the first few days of the war, Israel was close to defeat. But a massive airlift of arms from the USA, and fierce fighting from the IDF, saved the situation for Israel. The Syrian forces were repelled and the Egyptians driven back.

Whose victory?

At this point the USA and Soviet Union stepped in to stop the fighting. A ceasefire came into effect on 22 October. Both sides could claim victory: Israel had won the war, but from an Arab point of view only because it had been saved by the USA. The Arab states had shown that they could work together to fight effectively, and that they should not be underestimated. In particular, the war enhanced Sadat's reputation around the world. The war cost thousands of lives, but it opened up the possibilities for negotiations once more.

An Egyptian soldier holds up a portrait of President Sadat during the October War of 1973.

The Palestine Liberation Organization

In the years after 1949, there were times when the Arab states seemed more intent on furthering their own interests than those of the Palestinian Arabs, many of whom were living as refugees in the West Bank and Gaza Strip as well as in Syria, Jordan, Lebanon and Egypt. Most of the refugees longed for the day when they could return to their homes in Palestine. A few took direct action. Small groups of *fedayeen* ('fanatics' or 'self-sacrificers') launched guerrilla attacks on Israel. In the late 1950s, a group of *fedayeen* formed a Palestinian guerrilla organization called Fatah. One of Fatah's leaders was Yasser Arafat.

Founding the PLO

In 1964, Arab leaders decided to set up the Palestine Liberation Organization (PLO) to represent the Palestinian Arabs, and to bring together Fatah and other Palestinian groups in one organization. At first the PLO was largely controlled by the Arab states. But the outcome of the Six-Day War in 1967 (see pages 18–19) weakened Syria, Jordan and Egypt. Many Palestinian Arabs became convinced of the need to rely on no-one but themselves in the fight for their homeland.

Karameh

During the Six-Day War, many Palestinian Arabs had fled from the West Bank to Jordan. In the late 1960s, the PLO established bases in Jordan and organised guerrilla raids into Israel. The Israelis responded

To liberate Palestine

'Armed struggle is the only way to liberate Palestine.'

From the Palestine National Charter, 1968

with reprisal attacks. In March 1968, after a Fatah assault that had left two Israeli schoolchildren dead, the Israel Defense Forces (IDF) crossed the border into Jordan to attack a Fatah base in the city of Karameh. The IDF quickly ran into trouble as its troops met resistance not only from the Palestinian guerrillas but also from the Jordanian army. Although the IDF managed to destroy the Fatah base, 28 Israelis were killed and tanks and equipment abandoned in a hasty retreat.

While Israel could claim a military victory, Karameh was a turning point in the history of the PLO. Stories of the brave fight against the forces of the IDF boosted morale and inspired thousands of Palestinian refugees to volunteer for action. Despite being a small and relatively insignificant battle, Karameh boosted the prestige of Yasser Arafat and highlighted the Palestinian cause worldwide. Fatah emerged as the strongest group within the PLO, and in 1969 Yasser Arafat became chairman of the organization.

Israel will not disappear

'…the Arabs still couldn't, and didn't, come to grips with the fact that Israel was not going to accommodate them by disappearing from the map.'

From the autobiography of Golda Meir, Israeli prime minister 1969–74

Freedom fighters or terrorists?

After Karameh, King Hussein of Jordan had declared "We are all *fedayeen*". But as the PLO escalated its campaign of violence against Israel from bases in Jordan, King Hussein became increasingly concerned that he was losing control of his own country. In 1970, he ordered the Jordanian army to drive out the PLO. In the fighting that followed thousands of Palestinians were killed, and many more fled to new bases in Lebanon and Syria.

Arab fights Arab

The incident that led King Hussein finally to expel the PLO was the hijacking of five passenger planes by an extremist Palestinian group, the Palestinian Front for the Liberation of Palestine (PFLP), in September 1970. Three of these planes, from US, British and Swiss airlines, were landed at an air base in the Jordanian desert that was controlled by the PLO, and more than 400 passengers and crew were taken hostage. Although no hostages were killed, the planes were eventually blown up.

The Munich Olympics

Two years later, another extremist Palestinian group, Black September,

War of terrorism

'Last week, in the aftermath of the Munich murders, the Israeli government vowed to carry the war of terrorism back to the Arabs…'

From **Time:** *'Israel's New War' September 1972*

carried out an attack that shocked the whole world. Eight Palestinian terrorists broke into the athletes' village at the Olympic Games in Munich, Germany, and entered the lodgings of the Israeli team. Two Israeli athletes were killed as they resisted the terrorists; nine more were taken hostage. The Black September terrorists demanded the release of Palestinian prisoners being held in Israel. During an attempted rescue by German police, the remaining nine hostages all died. Five of the eight terrorists were also killed. The attack had a huge impact across the world, as it confirmed that such attacks were no longer confined to the Middle East.

Extremist tactics

What did the terrorists hope to achieve by such tactics? The argument of Palestinian extremists was that while raids into Israel had little or no effect, international plane hijackings and hostage-taking brought worldwide publicity for the Palestinian situation. In their view, Israel had committed an 'act of terrorism' by 'invading' Palestine. But while the Munich massacre certainly made headlines worldwide, the slaughter of the Israeli athletes attracted widespread revulsion. It also brought heavy reprisals from the Israelis, who bombed Palestinian camps in Syria and Lebanon, killing hundreds.

9 May 1972: armed police in Munich, Germany, drop into position on a terrace directly above the apartments where members of the Israeli Olympic team are being held hostage by Palestinian extremists.

Just cause?

'The difference between the revolutionary and the terrorist lies in the reason for which each fights. For whoever stands by a just cause and fights for the freedom and liberation of his land ... cannot possibly be called terrorist... '

From a speech made by Yasser Arafat in 1974 to the UN General Assembly

The 'Occupied Territories'

After the Six-Day War in 1967 (see pages 16–19), Israel sent troops into the territories it had gained during the war – the West Bank, the Golan Heights, the Gaza Strip and Sinai. They became known as the 'occupied territories', although many Israelis reject the use of this term. They argue that Israel won these territories in a war of self-defence, and that in any case Jordanian rule over the West Bank and Egyptian rule over the Gaza Strip were both the result of a war of Arab aggression in 1948 (see pages 14–15). In 1979, Israel signed a peace agreement with Egypt and handed Sinai back to Egyptian control. But the questions over the legality of Israel's presence in the West Bank, Golan Heights and Gaza Strip remained.

Israel imposed military rule on the Palestinian residents of the occupied territories. Daily life became difficult and uncomfortable for all Palestinians, as they were denied many basic freedoms. For example, any display of the Palestinian national flag or colours was forbidden, as it was seen as a threat to Israeli security. The IDF also rounded up suspected members of the PLO, which it considered to be a terrorist organization, who were then either deported or imprisoned.

Jewish settlements

Successive Israeli governments encouraged Jewish settlement in

No legal validity?

'… the policy and practices of Israel in establishing settlements in the Palestinian and other Arab territories occupied since 1967 have no legal validity and constitute a serious obstruction to achieving a comprehensive, just and lasting peace in the Middle East… '

From UN Resolution 446, March 1979

1981: a boy walks through the dusty streets of Kfar Adumim, a Jewish settlement in the West Bank.

Historic and religious connection

'Many present-day Israeli settlements have been established on sites that were home to Jewish communities in the West Bank (Judea and Samaria) in previous generations, in an expression of the Jewish people's deep historic and religious connection with the land.'

From the Israel Ministry of Foreign Affairs website

the territories. Israel acquired or confiscated land, particularly in the West Bank, which was then made available for Jewish settlers. The IDF built roads to link Jewish settlements. The pace of settlement speeded up considerably after 1977, when the right-wing Likud ('Consolidation') alliance took power in Israel. A plan drawn up by the first Likud prime minister, Menachem Begin, and his minister of agriculture, Ariel Sharon, called for the settlement of two million Jews in the occupied territories. Increasingly, Palestinian towns and villages were surrounded and separated by Jewish settlements and roads. In 1972 there were roughly 1,500 settlers in the West Bank and Gaza Strip; by 1983 this number had risen sharply to nearly 30,000.

First Intifada

In Arabic, *intifada* means 'uprising' or 'shaking off'. In December 1987, an Israeli man was stabbed and killed while out shopping in Gaza. Two days later, an Israeli army vehicle crashed into a lorry at a road block in Jabalya, the largest refugee camp in Gaza, killing the four Palestinian occupants. Rumours quickly spread that this accident was in fact an Israeli revenge attack, and rioting broke out. The Palestinian rioters made road blocks

Masked Palestinian youths use slingshots and stones to attack Israeli soldiers in 1988, during the First Intifada.

out of tyres and threw stones and home-made bombs at Israeli police and security patrols. The violence quickly spread from Jabalya, across Gaza and into the West Bank.

Israeli response

The Intifada took everyone by surprise. It was not started by the PLO, which at that time was based in Tunisia, but was a spontaneous mass uprising against Israeli occupation and the living conditions being endured by Palestinians in the occupied territories. When the violence erupted, the Israeli military forces were unsure how to respond. Their soldiers were well trained and equipped for warfare, but not for dealing with civil disobedience. At first they tried to smash the uprising with military might. Israeli soldiers used tear gas, water cannons, rubber bullets and live ammunition against the demonstrators. But television pictures shown worldwide of stone-throwing Palestinian youths being shot by well-armed Israelis prompted the Israeli government to put an end to the use of live ammunition, although it continued with a policy of 'might, power and beatings'.

Divided opinion

As the Intifada continued it became more organized,

with various PLO groups active in Gaza and the West Bank becoming involved. Thousands of Palestinians took part in acts of resistance against the Israeli occupation including strikes, huge demonstrations, boycotts and refusal to pay taxes. These actions drew worldwide attention to the situation faced by Palestinians in Gaza and the West Bank. The Intifada divided public opinion in many countries – notably in Israel itself and in the USA, where many Jewish Americans felt sympathy for the plight of the Palestinians.

Casualties

In the First Intifada (1987–93):

- around 160 Israeli security forces and civilians were killed by Palestinians

- more than 1,000 Palestinians were killed by Israeli security forces; over 200 of those who died were under the age of 16

- violence between the different Palestinian groups resulted in the killing of around 250 Palestinians suspected of collaboration with the Israeli authorities

Talking Peace?

For many people, both Israelis and Palestinians, the First Intifada showed that continued violence would not bring a resolution to the Arab–Israeli problems. A political solution was necessary to move forward. But there were many obstacles to overcome before the process of talking peace could even begin.

No compromise

'The Islamic Resistance Movement [Hamas] believes that the land of Palestine is an Islamic Waqf [religious endowment or gift] consecrated [declared sacred] for future Muslim generations until Judgement Day. It, or any part of it, … should not be given up.'

From Article 11 of the Hamas Charter, 18 August 1988

The Israeli government had always considered the PLO to be a terrorist organization and, as such, would not negotiate with Yasser Arafat or any of its leaders. It did not alter this position when Arafat announced in 1988 that the PLO would be willing to recognize the state of Israel, and renounce terrorism. But this announcement did change the position of the US government which, for the first time, announced its willingness to talk to the PLO.

Extremist views

Despite the momentum towards peace talks, on both the Israeli and Palestinian sides there were extremists who did not want negotiations to take place. In the late 1980s, a new organization called Hamas (Islamic Resistance Movement) was founded in Gaza. Hamas was far more militant than the PLO – its aim was the creation of a Palestinian state based on Islamic law. The emergence of Hamas was secretly encouraged by the Israeli authorities, who saw an opportunity to divide Palestinian loyalties in the occupied territories. But Israel came to regret this policy with the increase of violent attacks on Israel by Hamas militants in the 1990s. The growing popularity of Hamas and other extremist Islamic groups was

Enough of blood and tears!

'We [the Israelis] who have fought against you, the Palestinians, we say to you today, in a loud and a clear voice, enough of blood and tears... enough!'

Israeli Prime Minister Yitzhak Rabin, at the signing of the Oslo Accord, September 1993

1991–2 ground to a halt. But the election in 1992 of a moderate Israeli government, led by Yitzhak Rabin, opened the door once more. In 1993 secret talks were held in Oslo, Norway, culminating in a famous handshake on the lawn of the White House, Washington DC, between Yasser Arafat and Yitzhak Rabin. Two years later, Prime Minister Rabin was assassinated in Tel Aviv by a Jewish student. The student, Yigal Amir, was a member of an extremist Zionist organization that opposed any peace deal with the Palestinians.

one of the factors that eventually convinced the Israeli government to start negotiations with the more moderate PLO.

The first peace negotations held in Madrid, Spain, and in the USA in

Yitzhak Rabin and Yasser Arafat shake hands after signing the peace accord between Israel and the PLO at the White House on 13 September, 1993. US President Bill Clinton and officials from both sides look on.

Oslo Accords and after

The agreement resulting from the peace negotiations in Oslo was signed in September 1993. It became known as the Oslo Accord, and its main document was the Declaration of Principles. This is what was agreed:

- Israel would withdraw its troops from the Gaza Strip and the city of Jericho in the West Bank. There would be other withdrawals from further unspecified areas of the West Bank during a five-year period.

- There would be elections for a Palestinian Authority (PA) which would have self-governing powers in the areas from which Israeli forces were withdrawn.

- Issues of 'Jerusalem, refugees, settlements, security arrangements, borders, relations and cooperation with other neighbours…' would be discussed over the next five years.

In May 1994, Israeli troops withdrew from Jericho and most of the Gaza Strip. A second Oslo Accord agreed in 1995 addressed the issue of Palestinian prisoners, as well as providing for the withdrawal of Israeli troops from major Palestinian towns. Elections for the PA were held in January 1996. The PLO won the majority of seats, and Yasser Arafat was elected president of the PA.

Differing interpretations

Despite all these positive developments, there were many issues that remained unresolved. These stemmed from the different interpretations of the agreements by Israelis and Palestinians. There was nothing in the agreements to prevent further Jewish settlements in the occupied territories, but many Palestinians felt that new settlements went against the spirit

Dismantle settlements?

'We don't want to dismantle communities [settlements] in the framework of the interim agreement.'

Israeli Prime Minister Yitzhak Rabin in 1994, discussing the issue of settlements in the context of the previous year's Oslo Accord

Under occupation

'It was obvious that the people who wrote the document didn't live under occupation because a freeze on all settlements wasn't included nor was the release of prisoners… '

Hanan Ashrawi,
Palestinian politician,
on the Oslo Accord, 1993

A Palestinian woman at a protest against continued Jewish settlement in East Jerusalem.

of the Oslo Accords. However, the seizure of Palestinian land continued, as did the construction of new Jewish settlements and roads. Although Israel had withdrawn significant numbers of troops, many remained to ensure the security of the Jewish settlements. For most Palestinians, the establishment of an independent state seemed no nearer to being a reality. Many began to switch their support to Hamas and other militant groups.

STOP SETTLEMENT

33

The Second Intifada

On 28 September 2000 Ariel Sharon, the leader of the Likud Party (then the opposition party in Israel), visited the Temple Mount in Jerusalem. Surrounded by hundreds of riot police, Sharon and other Likud politicians marched up to the Noble Sanctuary, one of the most sacred places to Muslims (see panel).

Temple Mount

The Temple Mount is a raised plateau in the Old City of Jerusalem. It is a sacred place, particularly for Jews and Muslims. It was the site of the First and Second Temples, the holiest places in Judaism. Today many Jews choose not to enter the Temple Mount itself to avoid breaking religious laws. Instead they focus their attention and prayers on the Western Wall, a surviving part of the Second Temple. For Muslims, the Temple Mount is Al-Haram al-Sharif (the 'Noble Sanctuary'). It is the site of the Dome of the Rock, and the Al-Aqsa Mosque. The Temple Mount is controlled by the Waqf, the Supreme Muslim Council.

For many Israelis, Sharon's visit asserted the right of Jews to enter the Temple Mount. But Palestinians reacted to the visit with fury. They saw it as a threat to impose Jewish rule over Muslim-controlled holy sites. Violence broke out in Jerusalem, during which Palestinians stoned worshippers at the Western Wall, and Israeli riot police shot and killed six unarmed Palestinian protesters.

What provocation?

'What provocation is there when Jews come to visit the place with a message of peace? I am sorry about the injured, but it is the right of Jews in Israel to visit the Temple Mount.'

Ariel Sharon, on his visit to the Temple Mount

The Dome of the Rock on Temple Mount in Jerusalem. Inside is the holy place from where Muslims believe the Prophet Muhammad made his night journey to Paradise.

Violence spreads

While Palestinian frustration after the Oslo Accords had been steadily growing, it seems that Sharon's visit was the spark that ignited the Second Intifada. Violence quickly spread beyond Jerusalem. Just as in the First Intifada, there were bitter riots during which Palestinians threw stones and home-made bombs. But this time many Palestinian militants were armed with weapons, obtained by organizations such as Fatah and Hamas. Another feature of this renewed violence was an increase in the numbers of suicide bombings and other attacks against Israeli civilians. As the death toll mounted, Israel responded with raids and bombings on terrorist targets in the West Bank and Gaza.

Dangerous process

'This is a dangerous process conducted by Sharon against Islamic sacred places…'

Yasser Arafat in a television interview, 2000

The security fence

In response to the violence of the Second Intifada, in 2002 Israel began construction of a 670-km (420-mile) barrier to separate most of the West Bank from Israel. The Israeli government justified the construction of the barrier as the only way to defend its people from suicide and other attacks by Palestinian militants. In June 2004, the International Court of Justice in The Hague declared the construction of the barrier illegal under international law, but the Israeli government refused to accept this 'advisory' ruling.

Animals in a cage

'We have become like animals in a cage. We are surrounded in all directions. Before, you could go wherever you wanted. You could go in and out freely. Now it's gone. There is no freedom now. This is not a solution – this will explode. The wall will come down, just as the Berlin Wall did.'

Dr Mustafa Barghouti, head of the Palestinian National Initiative, 2003

The effect on the Palestinians

The route of the barrier, approved by the Israeli government in 2005, has been the cause of great controversy. Large areas of Palestinian land were included on the Israeli side. Palestinians believe that the aim of the barrier was to give the Israelis the opportunity to annex new areas of the West Bank, and have condemned it as a 'land grab'. The barrier has divided Palestinian communities, separating them from family, schools and farmland, and causing great hardship in many cases.

The impact on Israeli security

Since the construction of the barrier, the number of suicide bombings has fallen. According to Israeli sources the number of Israelis and foreign visitors killed by Palestinian militants in 2006 was 23, compared to 289 in 2002. As a spokeswoman from the IDF put it: 'The security fence was put up to stop terror, and that's what it's doing…'

(Opposite) The security fence is a mixture of 8-metre (26-ft) high concrete wall and 3-metre (10-ft) high wire fence, reinforced with ditches, coils of barbed wire, watchtowers, electronic sensors and surveillance cameras.

In defence of the fence

'Separation is a practical way to lower the level of violence, reduce the hatred, fear and distrust, and restore conditions for peace… If the fence means that the next generation of Israelis won't live with the constant threat of terrorist attack and the next generation of Palestinians won't live with the feeling of being occupied by an enemy, then peaceful coexistence between Israelis and Palestinians can become a realistic hope.'

Web journalist Lisa Katz, from About.com/Judaism

Core Issues

Throughout the Arab–Israeli conflict, the claims of both sides over the city of Jerusalem have aroused great passion. After the 1948 war (see pages 14–15), Jerusalem became a divided city: Transjordan (Jordan) took control of East Jerusalem (which included the Temple Mount) while Israel controlled the western part of the city. Israel declared Jerusalem as its capital in 1950. Despite various UN resolutions, Jordan did not allow Jews access to their holy sites in East Jerusalem.

During the Six-Day War in 1967, the IDF captured East Jerusalem. A few weeks after the end of the war, Israel announced its intention of integrating East Jerusalem back into the rest of the city. In 1980, the Knesset (Israeli parliament) passed the 'Jerusalem Law' which declared Jerusalem 'complete and united' as the capital of Israel, and guaranteed 'freedom of access' to the holy places of all religions in the city. This law was rejected by the UN on the grounds that Israel had acquired the territory by force. Most countries have also avoided formally recognizing Jerusalem as the capital of Israel.

Opposing views

Jerusalem remains a core issue in the peace process between Arabs and Israelis. These are some of the main points from each side:

● Some Palestinians question whether there was ever a Jewish temple in Jerusalem. But most people believe that there is plenty of archaeological evidence which shows that the Dome of the Rock is built on the remains of earlier Jewish temples.

The promise of Jerusalem

'This year we are here. Next year in Jerusalem.'

Words spoken at the end of the Jewish Seder (service or ritual) for Passover

This street sign, written in Hebrew (top), Arabic (middle) and English, symbolizes the complicated history of the city of Jerusalem.

● Most Israelis say that they will never agree to the re-partition of Jerusalem, and point out that only since 1967 when Israel took control of the whole of the city have all religions been allowed free access to their sacred places. Many Palestinians argue that Israel has no legal right to any part of East Jerusalem, and that they want East Jerusalem as the capital of a Palestinian state.

One open city

'The Palestinians have a vision of peace: it is a peace based on the complete end of the occupation and a return to Israel's 1967 borders, the sharing of all Jerusalem as one open city and as the capital of two states, Palestine and Israel.'

From an article written by Yasser Arafat for the New York Times, *2002*

The refugee question

The Arab–Israeli conflict has brought about huge movements of people, and created thousands of refugees. The question of refugees, and more particularly the right of Palestinian refugees to return to Israel, is another core issue in the efforts to find a peaceful resolution to the conflict.

Waves of refugees

Between 1947 and 1949, at the time of the creation of the State of Israel (see pages 12–15), around 600,000 Jews became refugees.

Palestinian children in Aida refugee camp, near Bethlehem, fill plastic bottles with water at a public tap.

These refugees came from Jewish communities living in Arab states such as Libya, Syria and Egypt, and from territories in Palestine that came under Arab control. The vast majority went to live in the new State of Israel, where they became citizens.

At the same time, thousands of Palestinians fled the territories that formed part of Israel. They went to the West Bank and Gaza Strip, as well as to neighbouring Arab countries. Many Palestinian refugees ended up in relief camps provided by the United Nations, living in cramped tents or huts and barely surviving on inadequate rations. After the Six-Day War in 1967 (see pages 16–19), there was another wave of Palestinian refugees.

Numbers of Palestinian refugees

- Jordan: 1,979,580
- Syria: 486,946
- West Bank 727,471
- Gaza: 1,167,572
- Lebanon: 436,154
- Total: 4,797,723

(Figures from UNRWA, Jan 2012)

Right to return?

Most Palestinians continue to assert their 'right to return' to their homes and land in Israel. They base this assertion on UN Resolution 194: '…refugees wishing to return to their homes and live at peace with their neighbours should be permitted to do so at the earliest practicable date…' as well as subsequent UN resolutions. The vast majority have not been given citizenship by their host Arab nations (with the exception of Jordan), but continue to live as refugees.

Many Israelis, however, steadfastly deny that any such 'right' exists. They argue that the Arab nations should absorb the refugees in the same way that Israel took in Jewish refugees after 1948. They also claim that the Arab states have deliberately refused to deal with the Palestinian refugee problem in order to evoke sympathy for their cause. They point out that for Jews who need refuge there is just one Jewish state in the world, whereas there are many Arab nations that could offer homes to the displaced Palestinians.

Two-state solution?

Even during the violence of the Second Intifada (see pages 34–5), efforts to find a peaceful resolution to the Arab–Israeli conflict did not stop. In 2003, US president George W Bush launched what he termed a 'road map' to peace between Israelis and Palestinians. The road map was a timetable drawn up by the 'Middle East Peace Quartet' – the United

Negotiated settlement

'Israelis and Palestinians have many differences between them. But there is only one way to resolve those differences – a negotiated settlement, not through unilateral steps.'

'Peace can only be achieved around the negotiating table. The Palestinian attempt to impose a settlement will not bring peace...'

Israeli prime minister Benjamin Netanyahu to the Knesset, February 2011 (top), and to the US Congress, May 2011 (bottom)

Bridges of dialogue

'Let us urgently build together a future for our children where they can enjoy freedom, security and prosperity. Let us build the bridges of dialogue instead of checkpoints and walls of separation, and build cooperative relations based on parity and equity between two neighboring States – Palestine and Israel – instead of policies of occupation, settlement, war and eliminating the other.'

From a speech by President Mahmoud Abbas to the UN, September 2011

Palestinians at the UN

In September 2011 the Palestinian president, Mahmoud Abbas, formally requested to join the United Nations as a member state. He based this independent Palestinian state on the 1967 borders, with East Jerusalem as its capital. Abbas and other Palestinians say that they have been forced to take this measure because of the lack of progress in the peace talks with Israel.

Israel's response

Israel has already in principle indicated its willingness to accept a Palestinian state. But the Israeli Prime Minister, Benjamin Netanyahu, described the Palestinians' idea of using the 1967 borders as 'unrealistic'. He said that much has changed on the ground since 1967, not least the thousands of Israeli settlers who now live in the West Bank and East Jerusalem. As well as the precise location of borders, numerous other questions remain to be resolved, notably the 'right of return' of Palestinan refugees. Many Israelis fear that the return of millions of Arab Palestinians would effectively destroy the Jewish state.

Nations, the European Union, the United States and Russia – and it aimed to achieve an independent Palestinian state living side-by-side with Israel in peace. This two-state solution has been pursued ever since.

(Opposite) **2007: Israeli Prime Minister Ehud Olmert chats to school children at a mixed Jewish–Arab school in Ramle, Israel. There are several projects in Israel to educate Jewish and Arab children alongside each other, with the aim of promoting tolerance, mutual respect and understanding between the two communities.**

The end of this painful conflict still lies in the future.

Glossary

airlift an organized delivery of supplies by air when surface routes are blocked, often in an emergency

annex of a territory, to incorporate into an existing state or country

anti-Semitism hostility, prejudice or discrimination against Jews

arid very dry

boycott to refuse to buy a product or take part in an activity as a means of expressing disapproval

collaboration working together, co-operation

diaspora the scattering of people away from a homeland; for Jews the dispersal of Jewish communities during the Roman era

discrimination treating an individual or community unfairly because of their age, disability, race, religion or sexuality

embargo to forbid business and trade with a particular country

fedayeen Palestinian militants (literally, 'fanatics' or 'self-sacrificers')

genocide the deliberate and organized destruction of a racial, political or cultural group

guerrilla a member of a military group outside the regular army

High Commissioner a chief representative of one country in another country

Holocaust the Nazi genocide of European Jews during World War II

immigration permanent settlement in a different country

intifada Arabic for 'uprising' or 'shaking off'; specifically the Palestinian uprisings in the 1980s and '90s

mandate permission to do something

massacre mass killing

militant an aggressive or extremist person

mobilize to assemble or prepare for war

nationalism devotion or loyalty to a particular state or nation

Nazi Party the National Socialist German Workers' Party, founded in Germany in 1919 and brought to power in 1933 under Adolf Hitler

Ottoman Empire Turkish Empire founded in 1299 that lasted until 1923

partition the division of something into parts

persecution the act of harassing or hurting someone on the basis of age, disability, race, religion or sexuality

reprisal retaliation

suicide bombing an attack in which a person sets off a bomb that kills them and anyone close to them

superpower during the Cold War, the two superpowers were the United States and the USSR (Soviet Union)

synagogue a Jewish place of worship

terrorist someone who uses terror as a weapon

United Nations (UN) an international organization that was formed in 1945 to promote peace and international cooperation and security

Yom Kippur the Jewish Day of Atonement, the holiest day in the Jewish calendar

Further information

Books

Access to History: Crisis in the Middle East: Israel and the Arab States 1945-2007 by Michael Scott-Baumann, Hodder Education, 2009

Atlas of Conflicts: The Arab–Israeli Conflict by Alex Woolf, Watts, 2004

Questioning History: The Arab–Israeli Conflict by Cath Senker, Wayland, 2008

Secret History: Conflict in the Middle East by David Abbott, Watts, 2010

Understanding the Holy Land: Answering Questions about the Israeli–Palestinian Conflict by Mitch Frank, Viking Children's Books, 2005

Timelines: The Arab–Israeli Conflict by Cath Senker, Arcturus Publishing, 2007

Witness to History: The Arab–Israeli Conflict by Stewart Ross, Heinemann, 2005

Websites

http://www.bbc.co.uk/news/special_reports/middle_east_crisis/
BBC website guide to the Middle East Crisis

http://www.fmep.org/
Foundation for Middle East Peace (FMEP) is a 'nonprofit organization that promotes peace between Israel and Palestine'

http://www.middleeastedu.co.uk/
Middle East Education provides excellent resources for learning more about the Arab–Israeli conflict

http://www.unrwa.org/index.php
Website of the United Nations Relief and Works Agency for Palestine Refugees (UNRWA)

http://www.palestinemonitor.org/
'Exposing life under occupation', told from the Palestinian point of view

http://www.sixdaywar.co.uk/index.htm
A website that aims to promote better understanding of the Six Day War

http://www.merip.org/
Middle East Research and Information Project aims to inform on politics, culture and society

http://www.jewishvirtuallibrary.org/
An American-Israeli enterprise with lots of information about Israel and its history

Index

Bold entries indicate pictures

Both Sides of the Story
SERIES CONTENTS

Animal Rights Different from us? • Without feeling? • Do they have rules? • A background to animal rights • Practising what you preach? • Meat, milk and mass-production • Factory farming • Good farming? • Animal products • Animals and science • Genetic engineering • Wild animals • Culling • The pleasure principle • Four-legged friends • Animals in entertainment • Hunting • Rights and wrongs • The way forward

The Arab-Israeli Conflict What are the historical claims? • Zionism and Arab nationalism • Seeds of dissent • The Jewish state • Victory or catastrophe? • At war • The aftermath • The October War • The Palestine Liberation Organization • Freedom fighters or terrorists? • The 'occupied territories' • First Intifada • Talking peace? • Oslo Accords and after • The Second Intifada • The security fence • Core issues • The refugee question • Two-state solution?

Cloning and Genetic Engineering What is genetic engineering? • History of genetic engineering • Human Genome Project • Transgenics • Cloning • Animal and human cloning • Research cloning • Genetic engineering in medicine • Genetic testing • Gene therapy • Embryo testing • Saviour siblings • Pharming • The future of medical treatment? • Food and farming • GM animals and crops • GM in our food • Wider uses of genetic engineering • Sport

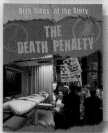

The Death Penalty A suitable punishment? • The view worldwide • How is it enforced? • The death penalty in history • The movement for abolition • Some religious views • 'Thou shalt not kill' • Retribution or vengeance? • Justice for the victim? • Life in prison • Does it stop crime? • Is it cost-effective? • Who is executed? • A poor person's punishment? • Race and the death penalty • Who should not be executed? • Case studies • Competency • Abolition or not?

The Ethics of War What is war? • The ethical arguments • The history of war ethics • Can war be justified? • Lawful authority • Humanitarian intervention • With good intention? • A last resort? • A good chance of success • Waging war • Pre-emptive strikes • Proportionality • Weapons • War and religion • Holy wars • Pacifism • Non-violence • Aftermath • War crimes

Euthanasia A matter of life and death • Different types of euthanasia • A noble end? • An end to suffering? • The practice of medicine • Life support • Mental anguish • Euthanasia and old age • The role of relatives • Safeguards and living wills • The role of religion • Do not kill? • Euthanasia and the law • 'Suicide tourism' • The 'slippery slope' • Palliative care • The uncertainty principle • A time to die? • *On Death and Dying*